"Do one thing every day
that scares you."

[Pastor IV Marsh[1]]

Introduction

Welcome to a 30-day journey that will transform your heart and mind—and your life. Welcome to a new day in your journey in God where you will learn to live EPIC.

God has called you to live an EPIC life, and he's empowered you to succeed because you are connected to a love that never fails—God himself. He wants you to know that you are not limited by your past nor are you to live intimidated by your future. God's presence is his gift to you to guide you on the way forward.

As you walk through this devotional, I believe that inside of you and all around you, you will change. The voices that once competed for your attention will be quieted by God's voice. He will draw closer to you in your weakness and show himself strong on your behalf.

As you read and respond to the daily calls to action, God will encourage you on how to retrain your heart and mind, and I believe you will find yourself stepping into places you never dreamed of going and doing things you never dreamed of doing.

For the next 30 days, trust your ideas, putting them down on these pages. Let them compel you to step into the unknown and outside the lines of what is familiar. See the days ahead as blank pages full of possibilities awaiting you to pen your decisions—waiting for you to take the first steps for a new and better future.

Let's get started. Let's learn together how to live EPIC!

IV Marsh

LIVE | EPIC DAY ONE

COURAGE is choosing to be seen when it feels easier to hide. To not be afraid to trust God beyond what you can see. It's finding the way forward and living and being epic, regardless of the discouragement trying to halt you. There is always a way forward, but fear will always be there wanting you to focus on the uncertainty, the disappointments, and the questions. Today, choose to give your attention to hope, possibility and to love.

Trust that your past has been overcome by the One who makes beauty from ashes; your future is secure in the hands of the One who created time. So, see yourself through the eyes of the One who created you.

He has given you permission to express, to rebuild, to create, to be unashamed, to experience something beyond what you have expected. He has given you permission to live epic.

Saying "yes" to living epic sets something so powerful in motion that it will reach beyond your lifetime.

> **"Now's the day and now's the hour."**
> [ROBERT BURNS]

Take a first step. Do one thing every day that scares you more than anything else. If you do, then you will discover that you have changed your world and the world around you.

Dream, Experience, and LIVE EPIC!

What are the things that scare you the most? Write them down, and commit to doing one every day until you have conquered them all.

LIVE | EPIC DAY TWO

The LORD had said to Abram, "Go from your country, your people and your father's household to the land I will show you."

[GENESIS 12:1]

This journey will require 2 things:

1) Courage
2) Faith

The place where most people miss it, however, is in the definition of those terms.

Courage is <u>NOT</u> the absence of fear, but it is living life in spite of the fear.

Faith is <u>NOT</u> "hoping it all works out," but it is a confidence in what we hope for and assurance about what we do not see. Faith is KNOWING that it all WILL work out.

What is it that you HOPE for? What is it that you desperately want in your life, but you do not currently see?

Now.
Display some courage.

What steps do you need to begin taking to make that dream happen?

Write down 3 steps to connect you with that dream.

Now.
Give yourself a date to have completed those steps.

"A journey of a thousand miles must begin with one step."
[OLD CHINESE PROVERB]

LIVE | EPIC DAY THREE

Immediately Jesus made the disciples get into the boat and go on ahead of him to the other side, while he dismissed the crowd. After he had dismissed them, he went up on a mountainside by himself to pray. Later that night, he was there alone, and the boat was already a considerable distance from land, buffeted by the waves because the wind was against it.

Shortly before dawn Jesus went out to them, walking on the lake. When the disciples saw him walking on the lake, they were terrified. "It's a ghost," they said, and cried out in fear.

But Jesus immediately said to them: "Take courage! It is I. Don't be afraid."

"Lord, if it's you," Peter replied, "tell me to come to you on the water."

"Come," he said.

Then Peter got down out of the boat, walked on the water and came toward Jesus.

[MATTHEW 14:22-29]

The fact that you are reading this devotional tells me that you want to experience a life of *MORE*. You want to experience more excitement and more passion. You want to live the life you have always dreamed. But when you look in the Scriptures, what you see time and time again, is that to experience an epic life, you must be willing to get out of the boat.

You must be willing to take that first step of faith!

"Behold the turtle! He makes progress only when he sticks out his neck."
[JAMES B. CONANT]

What did you do today to "get out of the boat"?

What did you do that was completely unlike your personality or outside of your comfort zone?

If nothing, then what will you do today that requires you to "get out of the boat"?

Now.
As Nike says... Just Do It!®

LIVE | EPIC DAY FOUR

Enter through the narrow gate. For wide is the gate and broad is the road that leads to destruction, and many enter through it. But small is the gate and narrow the road that leads to life, and only a few find it.

[MATTHEW 7:13-14]

As you begin taking steps on the road to your epic life, you will find that there are two paths before you.

One road is broad and well-traveled. You will see all the footsteps of the men and women who have gone before you. You will see where they have fallen, and you will see where they have slipped. The broad path is an easy hike. But you will find that it only leads you in circles, and you will never find the life that you seek.

The second path you will see, however, is rocky and steep. It is so difficult to see that it is almost hidden. It will not look like anyone has ever had the courage to follow the second path, but if you do, you will find that your epic life is just at the end!

Think about your life.

What is a path you have been avoiding because you thought it would be too difficult?

What is the path that you have been avoiding for most of your life even though you *KNOW* it is the path you should be on?

As you begin your day today, look for the narrow path.

Do not let fear hold you back, and when you see those small, hidden paths, take them and see where they lead!

Come back at the end of the day and answer the following: The path I took today led me to…

"Two roads diverged in a wood - and I took the one less traveled by, and it has made all the difference."
[ROBERT FROST]

LIVE | EPIC DAY FIVE

> **Do not conform to the pattern of this world, but be transformed by the renewing of your mind. Then you will be able to test and approve what God's will is—his good, pleasing and perfect will.**
> [ROMANS 12:2]

You are on your way! You are taking steps in the right direction, and you have made the decision to take the narrow path! But your journey to an epic life is just beginning.

To accomplish your goals and experience the life you so desire, there is another key ingredient: **Mental Strength.**

What the mind believes, the body achieves. Mental strength affects everything you do!

Being able to LIVE EPIC begins with being free to become all that God has created you to be.

> **Then you will know the truth, and the truth will set you free.**
> [JOHN 8:32]

Develop mental strength by doing these 6 things:

1. **Stay positive.**
2. **Breathe.**
3. **Have a short-term memory.**
4. **Hang around winners.**
5. **Visualize the future.**
6. **Set goals.**

"The price of doing the same old thing is far higher than the price of change."
[BILL CLINTON]

What are the "same old things" that you know you should change in your life?

To change your life, you must change the way you think. How can you change your thinking today?

LIVE | EPIC DAY SIX

> **We demolish arguments and every pretension that sets itself up against the knowledge of God, and we take captive every thought to make it obedient to Christ.**
> [2 CORINTHIANS 10:5]

You must be aware of your thoughts at all times.

> **Finally, brothers and sisters, whatever is true, whatever is noble, whatever is right, whatever is pure, whatever is lovely, whatever is admirable—if anything is excellent or praiseworthy—think about such things.**
> [PHILIPPIANS 4:8]

Never have an attitude of *"woe is me."*

As you go through your day, use "power statements" like, "I got this!". Use "power poses" like the Superman or Wonder Woman poses. If this is a little weird at first, then just STAND TALL!

Once you are choosing positivity, you must maintain that positivity by:

1. Being aware of your thoughts as soon as they try to go negative.

2. Intercept the negative thought, and then...

3. Replace it with a powerful truth. For example: "I can do all things through Christ."

4. Now, MAINTAIN with a positive power statement that you repeat in your mind over and over again.

"Think you can. Think you can't. Either way, you'll be right."
[HENRY FORD]

Today, I will think on:

Come back at the end of the day and answer the following: What happened as a result of positive thinking?

LIVE | EPIC DAY SEVEN

Then the Lord God formed a man from the dust of the ground and breathed into his nostrils the breath of life, and the man became a living being.

[GENESIS 2:7]

Would you just breathe!?!? **Just breathe!!**
Yes, the path is difficult.
Yes, there are dangers at every turn.
But you have to take time to breathe!

Controlling your breathing is vital to making it through any situation because in difficult situations, one of the only things you can control is your breathing.

Take heart, because regardless of what life throws at you, if you are still breathing, you are OK! If you are not breathing, then we have a problem *(seriously, if you are not breathing, call 911)*. But if you still have breath in your lungs, then you are fine.

Here is what happens:
Stress causes a reaction, and more often than not, that reaction is *FEAR*.

As living beings, we have 3 reactions to fear:

1. **Flight**
2. **Fight**
3. **Freeze**

Example:

STRESS > MIND & BODY = REACTION
(with no breath control, we will react emotionally, not rationally)

STRESS > MIND & BODY (BREATHE SLOWLY) = RESPONSE
(this creates a gap, which allows us to stop our reaction, allowing us to respond rationally)

> **"Courage is being scared to death and saddling up anyway."**
> [JOHN WAYNE]

Breathe and do not quit. You can make it!

Come back at the end of the day and answer the following: How did this help today?

LIVE | EPIC DAY EIGHT

Brothers and sisters, I do not consider myself yet to have taken hold of it. But one thing I do: Forgetting what is behind and straining toward what is ahead.

[PHILIPPIANS 3:13]

Now that you have begun this journey, you are going to find yourself tempted to look behind you.

You are going to be tempted to focus on what happened last year, or last month, or even what happened this morning.

But to experience your epic life, you cannot allow your past to dictate your future.

If you continue to drive through life while looking in the rear-view mirror, you will wreck.

Did you mess up?
Yes!

Did you fail?
Yes!

Do not waste a failure; learn from it and move on.

"I've come to believe that all my past failure and frustration were actually laying the foundation for the understandings that have created the new level of living I now enjoy."
[ANTHONY ROBBINS]

What past failures will you *NOT* allow to define you any longer?

Have a funeral for these past failures.

Write them on a piece of paper, place them in a "coffin," and burn them.

LIVE | EPIC DAY NINE

Walk with the wise and become wise; associate with fools and get in trouble.
[PROVERBS 13:20 NLT]

There is an old saying that says,

"Show me your friends, and I'll show you your future."

That is a very true saying, and it is a truth that you need to take very seriously if you want to live an epic life.

Now that you have made the difficult decision to take this journey, there is another difficult decision to make, and that is to decide who comes with you.

The company you keep will always determine the person you become. If you want to be a happy, joyful person, then it is impossible for you to surround yourself with sad, sorrowful friends.

Honest moment...
Some people are like clouds; when they disappear, your day gets brighter.

If you want to win, hang out with winners.
If you want to experience the best possible life, make sure you are not being influenced by the wrong type of person.

Who are some people you should distance yourself from?

Who are some people you should get closer to?

LIVE | **EPIC** DAY TEN

Then the Lord said to Joshua, "SEE, I have given Jericho into your hands, along with its king and its fighting men.
[JOSHUA 6:2]

The path you are on is difficult.
There will be days where you will want to throw in the towel. There will be days where you will want to turn around and run back the way you came.
That is where this next skill will become useful.

VISUALIZATION.

In order to live an epic life and be the best you that you can be, you have to learn to visualize both of those things.

You have to see your victory before you see your victory. You have to have a vision for your life.

If you do not see it before you see it, you will never see it.

To help you do this, answer the following questions:

1) What does the best YOU look like?

2) What does your dream MARRIAGE look like?

3) What does it look like for you to be the best PARENT?

4) What does the best FINANCIAL life look like to you?

5) What does your dream CAREER look like?

You really have to see it before you will ever see it!

LIVE | EPIC DAY ELEVEN

And the Lord answered me: "Write the vision; make it plain on tablets, so he may run who reads it.
[HABAKKUK 2:2 ESV]

To accomplish great things you must dream, you must visualize, and then you have to:

**PLAN.
BELIEVE IT.
ACT!**

Remember: What the mind believes, the body achieves. Yesterday, you visualized your best life, and you wrote down what that life would look like. The next step is going through a process called **REVERSE ENGINEERING.**

Now that you have a vision for your life, begin to work backward from that life to get to the place where you currently find yourself. Make sure to move in "bite-sized," achievable increments *(goals)* to get there.

Here is a tip: Always set smaller goals at first so you can build momentum.

Each time you achieve a goal, you are a success. As your successes begin to build, you will begin to see yourself winning the battle for your life. And every time you WIN, it will further diminish the fear in your life.

These "bite-sized," achievable goals may need to be pursued every hour, or every day, or every week. The point is to give yourself a series of achievable goals to create momentum in your life.

This will lead to a series of successes. And once you begin to see yourself as a WINNER, then failure will no longer be an option!! *(and neither is quitting)*

Write down the goals that will get you to your vision for your best:

1) YOU.

2) MARRIAGE.

3) PARENTING.

4) FINANCES.

5) CAREER.

LIVE | EPIC DAY TWELVE

For I can do all things through Christ, who gives me strength.
[PHILIPPIANS 4:13 NLT]

You have completed 11 days on your journey. **Celebrate!** At this point, chances are pretty good that it has crossed your mind to slack off a little bit or even quit.

Stay on this journey.

Don't quit!

Worthy pursuits are not taken lightly with an air of *"maybe I can do this."*

There is now no room for hesitation or turning back.

Remember: Pain is temporary; quitting is forever.

You probably have been "trying" this up to this point.

It is DECISION time!

Often times "try" is our escape clause. If I try something and fail, then I'm tempted to say it really wasn't my fault. Maybe it wasn't "my thing," or maybe there were other factors conspiring against me.

But if I attempt something and give it all I have, and THEN I fail, well, now I have to look at the possibility of my own limitations and deal with my shortcomings. I'll actually have to face the fact that I am not as capable as I thought.

In life, we don't want to deal with our limitations, so we shrink back and fly into most things with a half-hearted effort, all the while keeping our finger on the eject button.

Today, we put an *END* to that way of thinking.

> **"Try not! Do or do not; there is no try."**
> [MASTER YODA]

Come back at the end of the day and answer the following: Today I fell down and got right back up in this area:

> **"Inside of a ring or out, ain't nothing wrong with falling down. It's staying down that's wrong."**
> [MUHAMMAD ALI]

LIVE | EPIC DAY THIRTEEN

"Try a thing you haven't done three times. Once, to get over the fear of doing it. Twice, to learn how to do it. And a third time to figure out whether you like it or not."

[VIRGIL THOMPSON]

Make today a day of adventure!

Schedule time to try something you have NEVER done before.

Who knows... you might like it!

Come back at the end of the day and answer the following: I tried for the first time:

It made me feel:

Did you like it?
Did you hate it?
Would you do it again?

LIVE | EPIC DAY FOURTEEN

In the beginning God created the heavens and the earth.
[GENESIS 1:1]

"Just dash something down if you see a blank canvas staring back at you.
[VINCENT VAN GOGH]

We are all born creative.

The imagination of a child is an amazing thing. But something happens as we grow up—our creativity is often stifled and sometimes even destroyed.

Now, it is easy to just blow past that last statement while thinking that imagination is something for kids.

But with no imagination, there are no dreams. With no dreams, there are no visions. With no visions, there can be no "best you."

This may sound overly simple, but I want you to dare to create art today.

Draw, scribble, or doodle something right here, right now:

What were you thinking when you drew it?

What do you see when you look at it?

Do you dream often enough?

Carve out 5 minutes a day to be creative.
When can I do this?

LIVE | EPIC DAY FIFTEEN

Go, eat your food with gladness, and drink your wine with a joyful heart, for God has already approved what you do.
[ECCLESIASTES 9:7]

Often times because our creativity is destroyed, and needs to be resurrected; our sense of adventure goes away too.

Yes, you know what is coming.

I am not going to ask you to jump out of a plane *(yet)*, but I am going to ask you to take a baby step and open up the door to your adventurous side.

Today's challenge is to try a food you SWORE you would never try.

Today I will try these new foods:

Come back at the end of the day and answer the following: Describe your encounter with the "scary food":

"One cannot refuse to eat just because there is a chance of choking."
[OLD CHINESE PROVERB]

LIVE | EPIC DAY SIXTEEN

> **For this very reason, make every effort to SUPPLEMENT your faith with virtue, and virtue with knowledge, and knowledge with self-control, and self-control with steadfastness, and steadfastness with godliness, and godliness with brotherly affection, and brotherly affection with love. FOR if these qualities are yours and are INCREASING, they keep you from being ineffective or unfruitful in the knowledge of our Lord Jesus Christ. FOR whoever lacks these qualities is so nearsighted that he is blind, having forgotten that he was cleansed from his former sins.**
> [2 PETER 1:5-9 ESV]

Can the Bible get any more practical than that? It actually says, *"make every effort to SUPPLEMENT (add to) your faith,"* and it gives us a list of things to ADD TO our faith.

FAITH will save you, but DISCIPLINE will set you free.

It is *impossible* to be spiritually mature and emotionally unhealthy at the same time.

You can be mentally strong but emotionally weak, and you will fail.

You need to develop a peaceful mind!

Psalm 46:10 says, **"Be still and know that I am God."**

Between stimulus and response is TIME. In this time is your power to respond. In our response lies our FREEDOM.

How do you do this?

MEDITATION.

That simply means we are to listen deeply, absent of active thought.

> **May the words of my mouth and the meditation of my heart be pleasing in your sight, Lord, my Rock, and my Redeemer.**
> [PSALM 19:14]

FEAR—*false evidence appearing real*—causes us to make emotional decisions.

Think about it: Still waters run deep!

Think about a creek where the water is shallow. That creek is choppy and has rapids. But where the water gets deep it is calm and smooth! You know the craziest part? The water is still running at the same speed! The difference is that its depth yields calmness and peace.

You cannot be shallow in your life. At some point, you will have to develop deep thought so you can still your mind and emotions.

What verse will you meditate on today to create a peaceful mind?

LIVE | EPIC DAY SEVENTEEN

The light shines in the darkness, and the darkness has not overcome it.
[JOHN 1:5]

Just like roaches scatter when you turn a light on, negative stored emotions will dissipate when you bring them to the light and share them.

Therefore confess your sins to each other and pray for each other so that you may be healed. The prayer of a righteous person is powerful and effective.
[JAMES 5:16]

At Epic Church, establishing and maintaining relationships is one of our core values because we understand the importance of being emotionally healthy. We want you to have great relationships so you can be real with each other.

We accomplish that through multiple and various small groups.

Who are some people you can contact, or some friend groups that you can get in and build relationships so you can be TRANSPARENT?

What secret do you have that no one knows?

Start the FREEDOM process by simply writing it down and reading it aloud to God.

Next Step:
Find someone you trust (spouse/friend) and be vulnerable by telling them your secret.

LIVE | EPIC DAY EIGHTEEN

BE GRATEFUL TODAY!

An attitude of gratitude is one of the most important factors in controlling emotions because the opposite of gratitude is entitlement.

> **Do not be anxious about anything, but in every situation, by prayer and petition with thanksgiving, present your requests to God. And the peace of God, which transcends all understanding, will guard your hearts and your minds in Christ Jesus.**
>
> [PHILIPPIANS 4:6-7]

Grateful people are less likely to have mental stress and health problems in general.

Grateful people's lives are overall happier in every category. Embrace gratitude today.

Make a list of everything you are grateful for:

Task:
Make a "gratitude box." Then, every evening write down something that you were grateful for on that day. On Thanksgiving, get the box out and read the notes aloud.

LIVE | EPIC DAY NINETEEN

For God has not given us a spirit of fear and timidity, but of power, love, and self-discipline.

[2 TIMOTHY 1:7 NLT]

"Courage is the resistance of fear, mastery of fear—not the absence of fear."

[MARK TWAIN]

Fear exists in the gap between what we know is true and what we do not know to be true.

It is in this gap that False Evidence Appears Real (FEAR). What are you afraid of?

How can you close the gap between what you KNOW to be true, and what you DO NOT KNOW to be true?

Hint: The antidote to fear is faith. How can you let the promises of God fill the gaps?

How has this reduced the false evidence?

LIVE | EPIC DAY TWENTY

Generosity is a key component to living life to its fullest.

For God so loved the world that He gave His one and only Son, that whoever believes in Him shall not perish but have eternal life.
[JOHN 3:16]

God is generous. If you want to be like God, then you need to embrace generosity. You are never more like God than when you are being generous.

The problem with the idea of generosity, however, is that too often we focus on what we DO NOT have. Do not focus on what you do not have to give, but rather focus on what you DO have to give.

What are some things you can "give" today?

What is a one-time gift that you can give that will stretch your generosity level?

What is something you can consistently do that will stretch your generosity level?

LIVE | EPIC DAY TWENTY-ONE

If you want to live life to the fullest, there is a word you need to learn and grow to love: **DISCERNMENT**.

Discernment is vitally important to becoming the best you.

We are not talking about discernment so you can know something about someone else, but so you can discern something about YOU.

Here are 4 keys to developing discernment:

- Control your **ATTENTION**.
- Control your **BODY**.
- Control your **CONCENTRATION**.
- Meditate on **GOD'S WORD**.

At any point in time, you are one decision away from a different life.

Think about it. That "decision" is: What will you choose to exercise control over?

You cannot control life experiences, people, the economy, your boss, your spouse, or your family.

BUT...

You CAN control your breathing, what you pay attention to, what your body does, what you concentrate on, and whether or not you meditate on God's Word.

Practice discernment of you today and come back at the end of the day and write down your success in this area.

LIVE | EPIC DAY TWENTY-TWO

Educators and psychologists agree that the ability to focus attention on a task is crucial for the achievement of a person's goals.

The average attention span for an adult in 2013 was 8 seconds. If you placed an adult in a room with NO outside distractions, they could get their attention span as high as 10 minutes—and that's in ideal conditions.

Due to all the external stimulation that is in our world today, the average time someone can concentrate without being distracted is 8 seconds.

When your mind wanders, where does it go?

If discernment is the primary way to achieve the life we want, then it is imperative that we learn to control our attention.

Ask yourself: *"What am I giving my attention to?"*

You *MUST* become aware of your thoughts so you can determine what you are giving your attention to.

You *MUST* be able to focus.

What are some ways you can stop distracting thoughts so you can focus?

Finally, brothers and sisters, whatever is true, whatever is noble, whatever is right, whatever is pure, whatever is lovely, whatever is admirable—if anything is excellent or praiseworthy—THINK about such things.

[PHILIPPIANS 4:8]

LIVE | EPIC DAY TWENTY-THREE

You may not believe this, but it's true: You control your body; your body does not control you.

"What the mind believes, the body achieves."

This is true because the body is the vehicle, and the mind is the driver.

Do you not know that in a race all the runners run, but only one gets the prize? Run in such a way as to get the prize. Everyone who competes in the games goes into strict training. They do it to get a crown that will not last, but we do it to get a crown that will last forever. Therefore, I do not run like someone running aimlessly; I do not fight like a boxer beating the air. No, I strike a blow to my body and make it my slave so that after I have preached to others, I myself will not be disqualified for the prize.

[1 CORINTHIANS 9:24-27]

When your body runs the show, where do you go?

If you were to control your body, what would be different about your life?

Come back at the end of the day and write down how you controlled your body.

LIVE | EPIC DAY TWENTY-FOUR

CHALLENGE: Go as long as you can, and focus on this moment right now and nothing else...

How did you do? What distracts you?

If you allow yourself to worry about the future, you can easily become overwhelmed.

If you allow yourself to focus on your past, you *will* get stuck.

If you force yourself to focus on the moment you are in, things will become clear, and clarity is *POWER!*

> **Therefore I tell you, do not worry about your life, what you will eat or drink; or about your body, what you will wear. Is not life more than food, and the body more than clothes?**
>
> **Look at the birds of the air; they do not sow or reap or store away in barns, and yet your heavenly Father feeds them. Are you not much more valuable than they? Can anyone of you by worrying add a single hour to your life? And why do you worry about clothes? See how the flowers of the field grow.**
>
> **They do not labor or spin. Yet I tell you that not even Solomon in all his splendor was dressed like one of these. If that is how God clothes the grass of the field, which is here today and tomorrow is thrown into the fire, will he not much more clothe you—you of little faith?**
>
> **So do not worry, saying, "What shall we eat?" or "What shall we drink?" or "What shall we wear?" For the pagans run after all these things, and your heavenly Father knows that you need them. But seek first His kingdom and His righteousness, and all these things will be given to you as well. Therefore, do not worry about tomorrow, for tomorrow will worry about itself. Each day has enough trouble of its own.**
>
> [MATTHEW 6:25-34]

If you could minimize your distractions, what could you get done?

What could you become?

LIVE | EPIC DAY TWENTY-FIVE

Today, we are going to talk about **MEDITATION.**

Meditation is *NOT* something weird where you sit on the floor and chant, "ohmmmmmmmmmm."

Meditation defined:

"The discipline to listen deeply absent of active thought."

May these words of my mouth and this meditation of my heart be pleasing in your sight, Lord, my Rock and my Redeemer.
[PSALM 19:14]

It is all about learning to keep our mouth shut, our mind open, and listening with our whole being to what God is saying to us about us.

My sheep listen to my voice; I know them, and they follow me.
[JOHN 10:27]

Take 5 minutes and listen to God without any distracting thoughts.

What is God saying TO YOU about you?

LIVE | EPIC DAY TWENTY-SIX

You have made it this far! You are doing great! How many times have you wanted to quit?

> **"Remember that quitting is always an option—and it's the only one that guarantees a predictable result. Stay in the fight and everything is at risk! Quit, and you know what will happen...NOTHING."**
> [JIM BOUCHARD]

Remember wherever you go, there you are!

> **Forget the former things; do not dwell on the past. See, I am doing a new thing! Now it springs up; do you not perceive it? I am making a way in the wilderness and streams in the wasteland.**
> [ISAIAH 43:18-19]

Always be totally **PRESENT**.

The future and the past do not exist in the present.
The past is a memory.
The future is a notion.
By collapsing time to the present, we eliminate uncertainty and ANALYSIS PARALYSIS.

We have all heard people claim to be in the wrong place at the wrong time, but THAT IS NOT POSSIBLE!

You are either at the right place at the right time *(you are present)* OR you are at the right place at the *wrong time (your head was not in the game and you were not AWARE).*

In either case, the decisions you make at that moment will determine whether you are a zero or a hero.

When you practice total presence, you will always have the clarity for right thoughts, and right thoughts ALWAYS lead to right decisions.

Right thoughts = Right decisions

Putting it simply: **PAY ATTENTION!**

When have wrong thoughts robbed you of right decisions?

LIVE | EPIC DAY TWENTY-SEVEN

Let's get REALLY focused. TOTALLY COMMITTED.

Total commitment is to focus at the exclusion of everything else. Once totally committed to an action or goal you put ALL your mental, emotional, physical, and spiritual energy into that thing.

> **Therefore, since we are surrounded by such a great cloud of witnesses, let us throw off everything that hinders and the sin that so easily entangles. And let us run with perseverance the race marked out for us, fixing our eyes on Jesus, the pioneer and perfecter of faith. For the joy set before him, he endured the cross, scorning its shame, and sat down at the right hand of the throne of God. Consider him who endured such opposition from sinners, so that you will not grow weary and lose heart.**
>
> [HEBREWS 12:1-3]

Worthy pursuits are not taken lightly with an air of "maybe." There is NO Plan B!
No compromising.
No quitting!

Will it cost to be totally committed? Yes.
Will it hurt? Yes.
But...

Pain is temporary, and quitting is forever.

Most of us say, "I will try," and TRY is our escape clause. If I try something and fail, it wasn't really my fault. Maybe the project was too big. Maybe it wasn't really my thing or maybe there were some factors piled up against me.

But if I attempt to do something with ALL I have—I am totally committed—and I fail, then there is a good chance that I will have to stare at my own limitations and deal with them.

Personally, I do not think we are as afraid of failing as we are of succeeding.

> **"Our deepest fear is not that we are inadequate. Our deepest fear is that we are powerful beyond measure. It is our light, not our darkness that most frightens us. We ask ourselves, 'Who am I to be brilliant, gorgeous, talented, fabulous?' Actually, who are you not to be? You are a child of God. Your playing small does not serve the world. There is nothing enlightened about shrinking so that other people won't feel insecure around you. We are all meant to shine, as children do. We were born to make manifest the glory of God that is within us. It's not just in some of us, it's in everyone. And as we let our own light shine, we unconsciously give other people permission to do the same. As we are liberated from our own fear, our presence automatically liberates others."**

[MARIANNE WILLIAMSON]

Write down what you will decide to be totally committed to.

LIVE | EPIC DAY TWENTY-EIGHT

Do you ever wonder what God's plan is for your life?

"For I know the plans I have for you," declares the Lord, "plans to prosper you and not to harm you, plans to give you hope and a future."
[JEREMIAH 29:11]

If God's plan is to prosper me—not harm me—to give me a hope and a future, why does it seem so hard to find that?

Most people never read the rest of the verse and just wander through life never experiencing the life God has for them.

"You cannot find what you do not seek. You cannot grasp what you do not reach. Your dreams won't come to your front door. You have to take a leap if you want to soar."
[CORY BOOKER]

God says in Jeremiah 29:13, **"You will seek me and find me when you seek me with all your heart."**

"With all your heart" means totally committed, totally focused, distraction-free, controlling your attention, controlling your body, maintaining mental toughness, keeping emotional control and always possessing a never quit attitude.

When you live an epic life with all your heart, THEN you will find and see the plan He has for you.

The reason most people never LIVE EPIC is that they find it too difficult and quit, *sadly*, right before they experience something GREAT.

"He turns not back who is bound to a star."
[LEONARDO DA VINCI]

What are you willing to do to know God's plan for your life?

LIVE | EPIC DAY TWENTY-NINE

When you die...die on E. That means EMPTY.

> **For whoever wishes to save his life will lose it; but whoever loses his life for My sake will find it. For what will it profit a man if he gains the whole world and forfeits his soul?**
> [MATTHEW 16:25-26]

I love this quote from D.H. Lawrence:

"Life is ours to be spent not to be saved."

You have 4 things that you have been entrusted with that only you can give:

1. Time. Your life is made up of 86,400 seconds in each day. The question is: *What will you do with those to make a difference?*

2. Talent. You have a natural talent that you were born with that no one else has. They may have the same "talent," but they cannot do it like you do it. This is usually how people make a living.

3. Gift. This is what is absolutely unique to you. You have had people say, "You are so gifted at_____."

4. Money. You have been given the opportunity to leverage money to grow God's Kingdom and to take care of your family and to bless people. We all need to understand that we NEVER "spend" money, but rather we are always sowing.

Don't be misled—you cannot mock the justice of God. You will always reap what you sow.
[GALATIANS 6:7 NLT]

Your life is made up of the sum total of what you do with these 4 things.

How can you redirect these 4 things to live life to the fullest?

LIVE | EPIC DAY THIRTY

Your talent is often what you are paid to do.
Your gift is what you wish you could get paid to do.
Put these two together and you LIVE your DREAM...

LIVE EPIC!

Most people never understand that it is possible to live their dream. Living your dream is where your career *(what you get paid to do)* is the same as what you are "called" to do.

If you will stay on this journey, and continue to surrender EVERYTHING to God, you will live the most EPIC life you have ever imagined.

What do you wish you could get paid to do—your dream job?

What are some steps that you can take to monetize that?

Now make the appropriate steps to accomplish THAT!!

GO.

LIVE. EPIC.

LIVE | EPIC

Pastor IV Marsh is the lead pastor of Epic Church. His passion is to see people experience LIFE and live it to the fullest.

With a raw and unfiltered approach to preaching, Pastor IV loves to see people engage God in fun and creative ways, and he has a unique ability to take complex ideas and present them in a way that they become simple and practical. He is hyper-focused on seeing our culture return to God's original creative order.

Married to the love of his life, Bené, they live in Decatur, Alabama, have two sons, Garret and Joshua, a daughter, Ella, and together they lead Epic Church and its multiple campuses.

You can connect with Pastor IV Marsh here:

Twitter: @ivmarsh

Instagram: @iv.marsh

Facebook: facebook.com/ivmarsh1

[1] *A quote often attributed first to Eleanor Roosevelt though spoken by many.*

All scripture is from the New International Version unless otherwise noted.

Made in the USA
Lexington, KY
29 July 2018